Sand

You don't have to
shout to Stand Out

thrive
on!

love,
Christine

Here's what people have to say about Christine Clifton and "You don't have to shout to Stand Out"...

Standing out in today's hyper-connected noisy world is more challenging than ever. Until now. Christine Clifton defines how to build your personal brand without shouting. Bravo! This isn't just a book; it's a manual to keep with you.

Bryan Kramer, CEO at PureMatter, TED Speaker, Best Selling Author of Human to Human H2H & Shareology.

As a fellow introvert, Christine's message of embracing and leveraging the strengths inherent in my personality type to connect authentically with others in business and my personal life really resonates. I wish I'd had this book when I started my business! Christine's guide is a tremendous tool that can increase results and help you to align your strategies with your unique style. A must read for every entrepreneur who struggles to stand out.

Kathy Ryan, Founder, Pinnacle Leadership Institute, Author of "You Have to Say the Words"

Christine's new book provides great tips not only for introverts, but also for those of us who consider ourselves extraverts! It's important to remember we don't all have the same communication style and you would be well-served by reading this book before your next networking event.

Maria Semple, CEO, The Prospect Finder, Author of "Magnify Your Business"

I'm really happy that Christine boiled down her vast experience and handed it to me on a silver platter via this book! She even mixed in the relevant scientific research. Thank goodness I don't have to go on making the same communication mistakes any longer. While I was reading I had to stop several times to make notes because I kept thinking of specific ways of how I could adjust my own communication to grow my business. This book is a real gem!

Chris Curran, Founder, Fractal Recording, Author of "Leap Beyond Your Limits"

I'm the classic introvert: I would rather do anything than go to a networking event. I'm also very action oriented. If you know that your purpose requires that you leave your house and get out in the world more, then Christine's book is a must read. It gives guidance and support that allows me to be me, be my purpose, and have real conversations that I enjoy (and I'm doing it all as I'm networking)."

Jennifer Urezzio, Author of "Soul Language" and "A Little Book of Prayers"

How will success find you? If you have a purpose, passion and presence and are willing to be an empathetic and compassionate partner, all you need to be is YOU! Christine Clifton provides a guide to success, but more important she provides confirmation that anyone can be successful no matter how unique they may be. Whether you are introverted, extraverted or somewhere in between, you can excel by simply taking action using the success principles outlined in Christine's book. Everyone deserves to be heard; it's your turn, no matter how quiet you think you might be.

Doug Sandler, Author of "Nice Guys Finish First"

In her book, author Christine Clifton gives great advice on how to position yourself to stand out in an already "loud" business environment. With a special appeal to introverts like herself, she suggests that "speaking confidently, calmly, and convincingly to the right people" is the best formula. She offers a "how to" approach that will not only help introverts, but any business person looking to differentiate themselves and make valuable business connections.

Bonnie Marcus, Author of "The Politics of Promotion"

"You don't have to Stand Out shout"

Networking Conversations
that Inspire Interest and
Create Connections

Christine Clifton

TECHNIQUES FROM A QUIET ENTREPRENEUR

Mindful Business Press
NEW JERSEY

You don't have to shout to Stand Out
Networking Conversations that Inspire Interest and Create Connections
Techniques from a Quiet Entrepreneur
By Christine Clifton

ISBN: 978-0-9987107-4-7
Library of Congress Control Number Pending

Author Photograph @2016 by Alyssa Polcek-Peek

Christine Clifton
Mindful Business Matters
Madison, New Jersey
christine@christineclifton.com, christineclifton.com
(201) 738-7463

Mindful Business Press
NEW JERSEY

Requests for permission or futher information should be addressed to:
Mindful Business Press
christine@christineclifton.com

Dedication

To Michele Grace.

Because you are. Grace. Pure Grace. Because of you, I am the (wyrd) woman I am today. Without you, this book wouldn't have come into the world..... and I wouldn't be driving a 2014 Spice Orange MINI Cooper Convertible! No words are adequate; I know you feel my heart.

● ● ●

To my clients.

Thank you for your vulnerability and courage. You allow me to see the depth of your soul's calling and trust me to evoke your authentic voices so that you can impact the world in a greater way.

I am in your debt as your openness enables me to further develop my body of work so that I, too, may more greatly impact the world. That integrated connection represents our role as individual threads in the colorful tapestry of the Universe.

I am eternally grateful.

You don't have to shout to Stand Out

Table of Contents

Foreword

"To Be an Entrepreneur Is to Be
Fully Human." — Gene Bohensky

I met Christine while I was first starting my coaching
and consulting practice, during—you guessed it—
networking. But not just any networking. The kind of
networking where even though you think you know
what you are doing, you walk into a room of people and
you realize you really have no idea where to start.

For an experienced business owner, a somewhat successful technical sales manager and serial entrepreneur,
I was way out of my comfort zone. I didn't know at the
time that I was the kind of beginner that didn't even
know there was a beginning yet. And here I was, going
out into the world trying to connect with people, trying
to get my first clients as a coach. It was discomforting.
It was humiliating. It was frightening. It was humbling.

Deciding to start your own coaching and consulting
business—or really any business—after spending signifi-
cant time in the corporate world is like deciding to go
through a door of complete independence. As you walk
through that door your life changes—for you are now

responsible for everything. No excuses. You have to get your own clients. You decide what products or services you will provide and what to charge for them.

Only you can decide what you are going to say about them and about yourself. Most of all you have to decide what you stand for, for YOU are now solely responsible for your success or failure, and it's going to take everything you have. If you are lucky, you will reach down deep and find your secret well of activation energy that so few ever tap, and use it to survive. That's true independence, true freedom, and what it's like to be fully human—risks and all.

The good news is that there are masters, people who have gone through that door and have learned how to thrive. They serve as goalposts for the rest of us, and they show us how to get there faster when we decide to set sail on that learning curve. And what a learning curve that is. Christine is such a master. Her work in this book is a culmination of her experience, her success and failures, solid research, and most of all the wisdom she collected on her long journey to successful entrepreneurship.

She's made it possible for me to turn meetings that might be successful into meetings that will definitely be successful. I've gained clients by using her approach and I credit her with a lot of the confidence that I've gained.

I have learned much from her, and have discovered that the methods and processes she describes here have a universal character. As they have helped me, they will help you, too, on your journey—only with Christine's help and advice it won't take you as long! Most of all, she cares about her clients and their success.

Gene Bohensky
President, The Alternative Board of Northern NJ®

Connect with Christine at these links

Join our community by registering here:
www.NoShoutStandOut.com

Join our Facebook Group:
www.facebook.com/groups/NoShoutStandOut/

Get some additional support:
www.MindfulBusinessMatters.com/Shop

Schedule a free chat with Christine:
www.ChatWithChristine.com

Introduction

Introduction

Before I can tell my life what I want to do with it, I must listen to my life telling me who I am. — Parker J. Palmer

I was winding down my time in 4th grade at St. Peter's Catholic School when my teacher, Mrs. O'Donoghue, held a class recognition event. She acknowledged each and every student by sharing a specific situation the student had experienced during the school year. Each recognition she made was accompanied by a small token or talisman. When she got to me, she was holding a small baggie of peppermint candies.

She proceeded to give me accolades for holding my composure during the school's Christmas concert: I was at the front of the church singing a solo—a song about Jesus to the tune of "Jingle Bells"—when my voice cracked. I simply stopped, cleared my throat, and continued singing. I don't remember feeling embarrassed or afraid; I simply regrouped and continued on. I also didn't think there was anything particularly special about what had happened. Apparently, she did —and the peppermint candies honored my throat-clearing incident.

I didn't originally have this story as the lead-in to this book. But it popped into my mind as I was finalizing my edits and I felt led to include it. As I was attempting to recall the spelling of Mrs. O'Donoghue's name, I looked in the "School Days" scrapbook that my mom kept throughout our childhood and I found the concert program still tucked away there.

Now looking at it, I do find it remarkable: that an introverted 9-year old child had the composure to get up in front of her whole school and sing a song—solo! Interesting, right? Interesting that I hadn't recalled that experience. Interesting that I didn't remember I was told I was special way back then. Interesting that it didn't feel special at the time.

We each have our own unique path in life, yet we often don't realize how unique we are. We just move through our lives, being who we are. If we're lucky enough, we'll find a mentor, teacher, friend, or coach who shows us what is special about us. Not everyone has had that luck in their lives, but I sure hope that eventually everyone will.

A business coach once told me that I'm not any different—but I *am* special. Initially I bristled at her comment. Of course I was different—I've felt like a misfit much of my life! Yet, the more I understood what she was saying—that the work I did wasn't any different than others like me—the more I was able to see my uniqueness. Not the uniqueness of my business, service, or work but the uniqueness of who I am as a person—THAT is my specialness.

Why didn't I realize this earlier in life? I have a feeling that at a very young age, many of us probably did. Our parents and family may have told us how great we were, just like Mrs. O'Donoghue did for me. Yet, at the same time, I think that many of us were cultured to fit in. Once we hit primary education, we're guided to sit down and be quiet. Kids teased other kids who weren't like them. For some, that teasing may have even turned into bullying. I was probably lucky that Mrs. O'Donoghue took the time to call out something special about me. For some reason, it didn't stay with me, though. Some felt conspicuous or ashamed about being different. So we tried to fit in.

I did my best to fit in throughout my professional life as well. As an introvert, I'm naturally skilled at observation. As a social introvert, I'm not shy and I could tell pretty quickly what I needed to do or say in a given scenario with certain people. It served me quite well as I rose quickly in the ranks of the companies that employed me. After 20 years, I reached that pinnacle six-figure salary and five-figure bonus. And my health suffered. I didn't realize how stressful it was on my body, mind, and spirit to try to fit in all the time; to feel afraid to be myself.

When I became an entrepreneur and began to learn how to promote myself in that environment, I found that I could be more of myself and that I could bring out my specialness—who I really am as a person. Many other entrepreneurs saw what I was doing and wanted to learn how for themselves. This interest afforded me the opportunity to go back and map out what I had done for myself and create teaching material so that I could help others.

When I work with my clients, it's not about replicating MY path; it's about using the architecture for my success and helping others apply it to their specialness so they can create their own successful, unique path—whether it's in their career, life, or business.

The sensationalism of promotion today—marketing or selling yourself or your business—just keeps getting louder. Our technology platforms and media onslaught subject us to a consistent stream of noise and sensationalism. Many promoters choose to get louder so they're heard above all of that noise. So things just keep getting louder and louder and louder.

What's the solution? Whisper. Well, maybe not literally whisper, but instead get less loud: speak confidently, calmly, and convincingly to the right people. You don't have to shout to Stand Out. All you have to do is invest a little time to purposefully develop your approach and then intentionally implement it.

If you're more introverted, like me, you'll likely strongly resonate with the mindful approach covered in this book. If you're more extraverted, you may not—as your natural style typically likes to shoot from the hip. Regardless of which style you are, you will gain a great understanding from the material in this book to inspire your listeners to action.

When any of us helps others understand how we like to be communicated with, and communicate to them in a way they prefer, it helps everyone feel more at ease. You've heard of the Golden Rule, "Do unto others as you would have them do unto you?" Some call this new approach the Platinum Rule because you're treating others the way *they* want to be treated. Or, more specifically, speaking to them in their "language."

No matter where you are on the introvert/extravert spectrum, I believe you're responsible for communicating yourself if you want to make a difference. The world is a lesser place without your voice in it. Whether you lead a business team, own a business, are a parent, work in corporate, or are in job search, you will be more successful when you are able to communicate in a compelling way.

The application of these concepts for the purpose of this book is a networking environment. I've chosen that scenario because most of my clients (and me at one time) report that they often don't know what to say or do to get noticed in the "sea of sameness" at networking events. Or they find themselves feeling embarrassed that they're rambling when answering that dreaded networking question: "What do you do?" Or they feel uncomfortable networking in large groups of people. Or their minds go blank when they stand up to give their elevator pitch.

While I'm a quiet entrepreneur, the concepts I present here apply to any business person who wants to build their network. In each section, I've given examples that apply to entrepreneurs and business owners, job seekers, and corporate professionals and leaders. If you're in any of these groups then you know the value of a strong network, which I call "kindred spirits." These techniques will help you inspire interest and create connections with your kindred spirits through engaged networking conversations.

So what IS networking? Many people define it as a place that you go. I don't. I define it as an activity that you choose. If you read the definition of networking from Merriam-Webster, you'll see my perspective:

> *"Networking: the exchange of information or services among individuals, groups, or institutions; specifically: the cultivation of productive relationships for employment or business."*

Nowhere in that definition does it say "an event you attend in order to sell yourself or your wares." Okay, I'm being a little funny there, but isn't that what you think it is? And if you think so, how many others think so, too? Aren't you ready for a different definition?

I invite you to shift your perspective of networking to be "the cultivation of productive relationships"—also known as finding your kindred spirits. By doing so, you'll see that everything presented in this book is applicable to any scenario where you're talking to another human being—in your life, career, relationships, business, or family.

It's important for you to know that I did not do the primary research for these principles in the book. I have a gift of seeing themes that occur in seemingly disparate places. Some of the research mentioned here is originally presented in different bodies of work, yet applies to the focus of this book. Other themes I share here come from my own (introverted) life experiences and what I observe in many of my clients. The people and work that influenced me are recognized at the end of this book.

I also consider myself an intuitive person who has a strong belief system rooted in "like attracts like." You'll hear this perspective, brought through what you say, on each of the principles. I believe that who we are as people must be brought into our work as well, as you'll see when you read further. I can't help but practice what I preach—I must, if I'm really being authentic. When we can't be our full selves at work, a part of us begins to atrophy and we lose our motivation.

I'm not saying we should try to convert others to our beliefs in our places of work, yet I *am* saying that it is essential that we are able to speak confidently and respectfully from our place of belief without judgment or criticism. This approach is how you find the right-fit people for your trusted network—those kindred spirits. You'll hear this "like attracts like" perspective throughout this book.

As you read this perspective, I invite you to interpret it in the language of *your* beliefs. Some of you might say "the law of attraction" or you know of the principles in "The Secret" or you believe "what you think about you bring about."

I use the words Universe, yet yours might be God or Nature or Higher Power or something else. At minimum, see if you can be open to the "like attracts like" concept in general and check in as to whether it resonates with you or not. You always have a choice, so feel free to take it, take part of it, or leave it.

I also believe in "karmic networking." For me, this means that if I'm being a resource to those I meet, I trust that what I give will come back to me. It may not come back to me directly from that person I'm giving it to, though. By taking this approach, it can help release expectations of reciprocation when you help others. When I receive something back unexpectedly, I feel delighted and know that karmic networking was at play on my behalf.

"Coincidence is God's way of remaining anonymous."
– Albert Einstein

In addition, several principles in this book are rooted in the brain science of decision-making and the behavioral science of motivation. I even throw in a little bit of human biology for good measure. I believe in harmonizing the practical and the intuitive.

Together with proven communication models and voicing your true self, you'll learn the art and science behind being heard so you can make great connections in your life and work communities. After all, you're likely feeling that draw towards greater fulfillment, which may have even influenced your decision to purchase this book.

If you're more on the quiet side like me, you enjoy taking the time to learn and implement new behaviors. We're readers, observers, and contemplators. Even so, the "shade" to that characteristic is that we tend to get frozen by inaction or analysis—especially when it comes to initiating interaction with other people.

My hope is that you'll begin to use the specific tips and techniques that you learn here and take inspired action steps—even if they are *only* baby steps—in your own life and work.

The Glory of
Communication

The Glory of Communication

*B*efore we begin, let's first take an objective look at what components make up communication (Source: Dr. Ray Birdwhitell):

Component	% of Communication	Medium Examples
Words	7%	Email/Text/Post/IM
Tone of Voice	23%	Phone/Audio
Facial Expression	35%	Video/Skype
Body Language	35%	In-person
	100%	

Words—Think about how our technology has transformed the way we communicate. Fax, then email, then Instant Message, then posting, commenting, texting, tweeting—the list goes on and on. In any of these mediums, you're getting across 7% of what you intend because you're just using words. This is why "emoticons" were born: to add feeling to our "just words" communication. :)

Tone of Voice—The phone was such a radical technology when it came to be. Imagine talking to someone across town without having to be there in person! Even with the added component of tone of voice, you're getting across 30% of what you intend. These days, you may not even remember the last time you used your phone to make a phone call.

Facial Expression—The evolution of smart phones has brought us things like Facetime to actually see the person with whom we're speaking. YouTube has transformed the way that we see the world. Skype and ooVoo have made video "calls" over the internet commonplace. By adding facial expression to words and tone of voice, you're now getting across 65% of what you intend.

Body Language—Ah, the good ole days! Many of our work environments today make it hard to get in person with the person we need to communicate with. Work from home arrangements, remote access, and business travel all impact this. While in-person gets across 100% of what you intend, your company or business process may inhibit your ability to use that option.

So, how can you make up for the fact that you're not in person or even in sight of the person you're speaking to? I don't believe that you fully can. However, like emoticons, you *can* find a way to enhance your chosen medium so that you're better heard—without shouting.

That enhancement is bringing in your own personal X factor, your secret sauce, your specialness, your unique position, the way you communicate, and the interest you take in others.

That's what I'm here to relay to you in this book: Four primary techniques you can develop so that your networking conversations interest others in you or your work and you're able to create great connections. The first two techniques help you inspire interest in your listener and the second two help you create connections with those you meet.

You'll also enjoy book bonuses that enhance your learning of each technique. There are free online worksheets that only those who have purchased this book can access. In addition, my guidebook is available for purchase to further support your learning of the techniques in this book.

It's called "Your Spirit at Work: Bring more of You, through what you Do, so your vision comes True" and can be found at www.YourSpiritAtWork.com. I've gifted purchasers of this book a $10.00 off coupon for my guidebook and for each of my digital programs that support further learning of specific topics (up to $60.00 total savings).

This book is packed full of information and the last section has ideas and examples for you to apply these techniques in real-life scenarios. Reading about new techniques is good. Learning them is better. Practicing them is best. After using these techniques, you'll feel more in alignment with who you really are so that you come across as confident, calm, and convincing when you network—and make great connections.

The Special Connector — Purpose

The special connector—*Purpose*

*F*acts. Figures. Logic. Practical. Proof. These are the things that I learned to present to my corporate colleagues in order to influence. Then, when it didn't work, I'd scratch my head and wonder what happened. In all those years in corporate, I navigated the politics and the different players pretty well, trying to figure out what motivated them—and it was exhausting.

As I transitioned into entrepreneurship, I now needed to motivate clients to hire me. In most cases, the politics weren't at play in the same way, but I still got caught up in the "figuring out" part. During one mastermind meeting that I hosted with other entrepreneurs, I shared a new business idea and why I was thinking about doing it. One of the participants said "Christine, if you decide to do that work, I'll be your first client." How's that for results?!

But, why did it work? Why did what I say cause him to feel so ready to decide? It was because I shared my purpose for doing the work. The purpose. Not the proof. You see, at that point, I had been an entrepreneur for several years. I knew what was challenging for me and for other entrepreneurs.

When I described my idea, I said that I wanted to alleviate that challenge for entrepreneurs so they could do what they do best—their craft. I had no track record of success with my idea. It was only an idea. A vision of what was possible. No proof, facts, or figures. I simply described my purpose for wanting to do it.

The question still stands: Why did it work? It was because what I said—my purpose—stirred an emotional response in the listener—and people make decisions from emotion, not logic. Here comes the brain science.

Our more primitive brain, the limbic brain, is where our emotions are generated. Before we had the ability to speak, we had the ability to feel emotions. All of that came from the primitive brain. Think caveman-meets-saber-toothed-tiger. The caveman didn't run a pro/con list in his head to decide whether to run or not. He felt either fear—and ran—or hunger—and fought. Fight or Flight. Emotion.

Even as we evolved and became more civilized—and began brain development that was able to produce language—that primitive brain has remained the same. It is what drives decision-making even in this modern day.

Remember all of that sensational promotional noise I mentioned earlier? Have you noticed the titles of viral videos, for example? "Here's the cutest kitty in the universe, and you won't believe what he does next!" Maybe you've noticed the headlines of your online news source? "Shocking new details revealed!" All of these titles go out of their way to cause an emotion in us so we'll decide to watch or read.

Now, we get to decide whether something sensational like that is in alignment with who we are. That is where your purpose comes into play. Your purpose isn't sensational, it just is. It's what motivates you to act.

Yet, it is even more powerful when you share it. You can't just know your purpose; you must articulate it so that others can hear it and make a decision if they connect with it.

How does this show up in the real world? It can be as simple as making a phone call to someone and starting the conversation by saying "The purpose for my call is." It can be more complex, like making a presentation to a potential customer to gain their business and saying "I'm here because I believe our product will change the way the world sees our industry."

It could also be as commonplace as me responding (as I often do) to that dreaded networking question "What do you do?" with sharing my Purpose: "I believe that everybody matters and deserves to be heard."

Simon Sinek, author of *Start with Why,* developed a concept called The Golden Circle. Within his body of work, he describes the brain science as I have here. He essentially says that people will connect with you "if they believe what you believe." The reason is that people buy Why you do what you do, not What you do. Again, they make decisions based on emotion—whether they feel connected to your Why—not logic.

Do you believe that everybody matters and deserves to be heard? Are you also an introvert? Would you rather not shout in order to stand out? Are you tired of not being heard? Do you long to make great connections with people? One, some, all of these? I'm going to guess that you do because you're reading this book right now. You resonated with my work on some level, realizing that you believe what I believe, and you chose to connect with me.

Once you know and articulate your purpose—Sinek calls it your "Why" (your purpose, cause or belief)—others will sit up and take notice…… or not. They will, IF they believe what you believe. Yes, you run the risk of them not taking notice. But, you know what? If they don't believe what you believe then you're probably not the best fit for them anyway. They aren't likely a kindred spirit.

Take a moment to think about your own situation: Are you in job search trying to influence an interviewer?

Maybe you keep getting passed over for promotions at work and you're tired of being overlooked. Perhaps you're a business owner at a networking event and don't feel any different than all the others there in your industry. Are you a business leader whose team isn't responding to your motivation efforts?

In all of these scenarios, you can stand out if you'll just articulate your purpose. *That's* what makes you special (not different). In the sea of candidates, colleagues, or business owners—you will stand out as special because *no one* has the same purpose as you do.

Having spent 11 years in Human Resources, I can't even count the number of interviews I was a part of. What I can tell you is that if someone had taken the time to look at our company mission and articulate their Purpose in a way that correlated with it, I would have taken great notice. Sure, we want qualified candidates. But I can tell you that jobs were more often awarded based on "fit" as a defining decision.

> *"Every sacred purpose is a buried treasure, essential to the advancement of the collective soul."* – Jeff Brown

Having an aligned purpose with the company is all about fit. If you show them that you believe what they believe, you will certainly stand out.

The same approach is true if you're in corporate and feeling passed over for opportunities. Find a way that you can connect with your boss's vision for your department and articulate to him or her that you're on board. If you're developing a project for the team, create a purpose statement for the project when you pitch it to others. When you host a meeting, cite the purpose so you keep the group on track to the shared vision.

As business owners or service professionals, it can feel hopeless to find a way to set yourself apart from the competition. You aren't any different anyway. It's your purpose that will set you apart, so take some time to think about WHY you're doing the work you're doing.

Then make sure that you're talking about WHY you're doing what you're doing. Ditch the dull elevator pitch and instead speak about your position on a popular topic in your industry. When prospecting a potential client, talk heart to heart with them about why you think you can help them.

The business environment has pushed most everyone behind a screen of some size. As a leader, your ability to connect with your team has been negatively impacted as a result. When people feel disconnected, their stress levels rise—as does the level of cortisol in their body because their fight or flight mechanism has been engaged.

Can you, as a business leader, tie your personal mission statement or vision to your company's? Could you facilitate your team to tie theirs to yours or the company's? If you can, you'll be showing them the Why connection and you'll gain more collaboration and motivation from your team—not to mention less fear and stress.

These approaches cut to the core of your listener's decision-making because it tickles their limbic brain. Knowing your purpose isn't just a feel-good concept. When articulated, it becomes a powerful draw to those who are like-minded. It also tickles *your* limbic brain and gives you the motivation to keep expressing your purpose. This alignment with purpose—and your conscious awareness of it—also helps you make decisions that are the best fit for you and that will allow you to keep expressing your purpose.

Stay in alignment. Speak from the heart. Share your purpose, cause, or belief. And those who are in alignment with you will pay attention. Don't worry about all the others who may not seem interested. There is likely someone else out there who is a better fit for them. Stay true to you.

Speaking your purpose is some of the strongest ground you can speak from. No one can debate what you believe. It's your position and that's a fact. It brings you the ability to speak with calm confidence—and THAT is compelling.

So how do you discover your Purpose? It is rooted much more deeply than just the work that you do. It is a part of your innate wiring. This topic may take a bit of your time to explore, yet is worth the effort in the long run. Most of my clients, after their Purpose discovery session with me, say that their whole life makes so much more sense. They are able to see their innate tendencies and strengths—and can now use them as a tool looking forward.

Go to www.NoShoutStandOut.com/BookBonus and use the *Purpose Worksheet* to prompt your thoughts about your Purpose. Make some notes. Look for themes. Your Purpose isn't solely tied to your work: it's an internal calling that shows up in all that you do.

"The eye can't see itself." I believe that getting help from someone else can evoke the most awareness of Purpose in the shortest amount of time because they see in you what you can't see in yourself. Talk it through with a trusted friend. Or you might choose to hire a coach who does Purpose work to help you.

If that feels like too big of a leap right now, you might watch Simon Sinek's TED talk or read his book or take his online discovery course. Another book on the topic is by Pam Slim called *Body of Work.* Parker J. Palmer wrote *Let Your Life Speak,* which I have read several times. Martha Beck also has several books on discovering your brilliance. The key here is to be curious and allow yourself to sense the right next step and resource for you.

Once you realize your Purpose, this calling that you're feeling, it will not only provide the energy behind your words, but it will also help you in your life decision-making. It's a beautiful side effect because you can now use your Purpose to ask yourself if an opportunity is aligned or if a chosen action demonstrates you in integrity. It's a litmus test of sorts and you can use it to check in with yourself regularly so that your path stays aligned with your calling.

When speaking your Purpose to others, it is also communicating to the Universe what your focus and intention are. I believe that like attracts like, so your emotional connection to your Purpose is what draws what you want towards you. When telling others, they hear you and either feel connected to you themselves or they will possibly feel inspired to connect you with someone else they feel would be a good fit.

With this connection comes cooperation and collaboration because we feel connected to something that is greater than us individually. It becomes a practical and intuitive tool toward inspiring interest and creating connections.

"Feeling more motivated than I had in a long time."

As someone very goal oriented, I was feeling confused as to why I didn't know what to do next to grow my business. Christine helped me see my natural strengths and tendencies—what my call to service really is. Then, she showed me how I could then use those consciously as a tool in my business.

I left that session feeling more motivated than I had in a long time. Thank you, Christine, for your talent, expertise and support! Without our session and the follow-up calls, I don't think I'd have this clarity with my next steps. I so appreciate you!

Janet Logan
My Coaching Services

The Compelling Messenger — Passion

The compelling
messenger — *Passion*

*W*hen I go out networking and I listen to elevator pitches, the most common first sentence I hear is "I help anybody who..." If I'm having individual conversations and I ask them who they help or who they want to be connected to they say "Anybody who...." "Anybody" is just too big of a pool of people and the listener simply checks out.

Another pitfall I hear is when people give their position title, like "I'm a financial advisor." The challenge with that approach is that it leaves the definition of that position title up to the listener. When the listener hears it, they will either silently wonder what that means (and never ask for fear of feeling dumb) or they will silently make a decision about what that means (and it will likely be wrong or based on a negative experience they had with that position title.) If you use this approach, you are disempowering your impact.

I also often hear people saying things like "we do everything...." Or "we're a print shop, we print stuff." Or "we're a community bank." While all of that might be true, it doesn't paint a picture for the listener of how you help them or how they benefit from what you do. It's all very "What"-centric and that doesn't inspire much interest in your listener.

I speak from total experience here, so don't think that I'm lecturing you. When you think about it, few of us were taught how to network. We're all doing our best, either picking up things from what we observe others doing or we're taught some of the traditional things about networking. The problem is that we are no longer in a traditional networking environment. Technology has changed us dramatically, as you'll soon read, and so must our approach.

The thing about those of us in service to others—as employees, parents, business owners, or leaders—is that we want to save the world. It's certainly admirable, but it's one huge job!

How do you eat an elephant? One bite at a time. How do you save the world? One group at a time. How do you serve "anybody?" One person at a time.

Imagine your entire set of skills or services or your company as sponge. The above approaches are an attempt to message the whole sponge. While people *get* what your sponge does, it isn't specific enough for them to realize how it will help them or others.

Instead, you have to message the divots in the sponge. The individual divots, or your separate skills or services, represent a solution to someone. By creating a specific message around one skill or solution is how you make what you say more interesting to the listener. It's a technique I call "micro-messaging."

Before I get into the specifics of the power of micro-messaging, it's important to understand how people are hearing us when we speak. The brain processes what we're hearing three to four times faster than the average person speaks. What that means is that when we're speaking to someone, they have a lot of processing bandwidth that they're not using. What that means is that they're making their shopping list, or thinking of tasks they need to do, or speculating on their next meeting—all while we're talking to them.

What do you think the attention span of a goldfish is? 30 seconds? 1 minute? 10 seconds? It's actually 9 seconds.

What do you think the attention span of a human being is? Did you laugh? Probably so. Stick with me here. More than a goldfish or less? If you guessed less, you guessed right. It's actually 8 seconds. You've likely heard that you have 7 seconds to make a first impression, right? This statistic supports that. You have mere seconds to catch somebody's attention.

An acquaintance of mine who is in job search told me she had a "screening" phone call recently. She said, "I've never heard someone talk that fast—ever!" Not to mention the fact that *she* was the one who was supposed to get screened and interviewed; there was hardly any time given to her to ask questions about the job.

Everybody's in a hurry. Our expectations have changed dramatically in terms of how quickly we expect something to take. While I do love technology, it is to blame, in part. You see, all those quick hits of checking our cell phone when it dings or scrolling through our email or Facebook or Twitter? Those actions are reprogramming our brain to scan instead of focus.

You know what else? We're getting addicted to the activity. Literally addicted. I mentioned Simon Sinek before and in his new book, *Leaders Eat Last,* he mentions how dopamine is excreted in the brain when we reach a goal and it makes us want more. Dopamine is what is activated in people who have alcohol and drug addictions. It's what makes them not be able to stop. We. Can't. Stop. Scanning.

As a result, when we're networking, we're interacting with people who have shorter attention spans than in the past. Add that fact to my earlier point about having extra bandwidth while listening. How in the world do we have a chance to get the attention of the listener?

It's by using micro-messaging. Now, don't get too caught up in the technical language. You can use Google and find some things about micro-marketing and possibly micro-messaging as well. The point is this: you must be super specific when speaking so that the person understands who you're talking about and how they benefit. Not "Anybody who..." The specific "Who" and the "Benefit." Let's break that down a bit.

When you say you help anybody—or you're being interviewed and you respond to a question with "I liked all my prior jobs,"—or you're talking to your boss in general terms—or your team is looking at you like "what's in it for me?"—you've lost your audience.

Who are the people you're really talking about? If you're an accountant, you're helping families or small business owners. If you're in corporate marketing, you're helping the salespeople. If you're motivating your team, you're helping the customer. The onus is on you to find the specific "Who" descriptor to relay to your listener. It needs to be so specific that it paints a picture in their mind as they're listening to you.

Now you're ready to add a benefit to your message. Think about the benefit to that person or group that you help. If you're that accountant helping business owners, you might be saving them tax penalties. Those salespeople? You help them increase company revenue. Those customers? Your team is building steady business for the company.

The accountant can now say:
"I help business owners avoid tax penalties."

The corporate marketer can now say:
"I help salespeople increase company revenue."

The business leader can now say:
"My team is growing sustainable business."

These are powerful micro-messages that quickly get the attention of your listener—because you're using words that matter to *them*. It is the first tier of a three-tiered messaging model that I co-create with each of my clients, which gives them the sound bites they need when giving their elevator pitch or while having networking conversations.

Here's one last example that most everyone can relate to: Jell-O®!

What is Jell-O® to kids? A fun, colorful, wiggly dessert!
What is Jell-O® to moms? A fast and easy dessert!
What is Jell-O® to college kids? A fun and festive beverage! *(Jell-O® shots for those of you who may not know.)*

The "What" (Jell-O®) is the same—but it "Benefits" the different "Who" in different ways.

Your "What" (business, career, service) is also the same. Yet, you do it for different people who value it differently. What you're doing/offering/selling means different things to different people. The power of this micro-messaging technique is when you "channel" the "Who", you can say the specific "Benefit" that only that "Who" cares about.

When you take your time to think through how "What you do" benefits the different "Who" that you serve, your messaging will hold their attention. By speaking in these micro-messages, you're painting a visual picture for the listener and what you say will be much more memorable to them.

It's a bit like the power of storytelling. Most of us learned as children the joys of listening to a story unfold. By getting super specific in how you relay your message, you are telling a story with specific details that makes others want to listen. Remember the brain science I introduced in the first principle, about people feeling connected emotionally to your Purpose? The same concept applies with micro-messaging.

When people feel as if "you get them", an emotional rise happens within them. When this happens, oxytocin is released in the body which is the "connection/collaboration" hormone. For those who resonate with your messaging, they literally can't help but feel connected to you because of this. Our biology simply works this way. It's not manipulation at all: it's your authentic articulation of who you help and how they benefit. The next action is up to the listener to decide.

Just like articulating your Purpose compels like-energy to be drawn to you, so does messaging. Messaging is your intention stated in words. How you message yourself is articulating your vision and desires to the Universe. I believe speaking is an action that begins to crystallize those beliefs in physical form, which brings what you want to you. Like attracts like.

Go to www.NoShoutStandOut.com/BookBonus and use the *Position Statement Worksheet* to brainstorm your position statements about your work. Whether you're in job search or are an entrepreneur, this will help you flesh out your unique perspective so you can use it when talking with others.

When I work with entrepreneurs on this concept, most of them raise one huge objection: they feel limited when focusing this specifically with their messaging. Remember what I said about saving the world? Yes, you can, yet it must be done one group at a time so that your messaging speaks directly to your Who's life circumstances.

Bring into your mind's eye your specific situation: Are you in job search? Are you looking to progress in your company? Are you a service professional or a service business owner? Are you a leader who wants to bring your team together for a unified cause? You might even be a parent who wants more connection with your children. Regardless of your situation, this concept of painting the picture for others with words works!

> *"Public declaration is the highest form of visioning." - Neale Donald-Walsch*

You might choose to use micro-messaging, or story-telling, or analogy/metaphor/simile, or testimonials/case studies. Leverage your communication skills by thinking through and creating these "pictures" so that your listener can *see* your point and *feel* connected enough to move to action. You don't have to force it, you just have to say it compellingly—this technique is what inspires interest.

"My leads and client base are steadily growing."

Before I worked with Christine, I felt very uncertain during networking, one-on-one meetings, and sales conversations. I knew how to tell people what I did, and I'm a very good copywriter/editor, but I didn't feel comfortable selling myself.

Christine helped me craft short sound bites that didn't feel sales-y. Now that I'm using them, my leads and my client base are steadily growing. It feels easy to talk to people and I'm getting more interest from prospective clients than I ever have before.

As a matter of fact, I got four leads at the last North Jersey Chamber Dine Around! I highly recommend working with Christine.

Susan Toth
Writing and Editing

The Temporary Chameleon — Presence

The temporary chameleon — *Presence*

*H*ave you ever had the experience of meeting someone for the first time and feel like they rub you the wrong way in the first few minutes? It can be easy to take the position that you don't like them or to believe that they're "doing" something to you. Alternatively, you may have had the experience of meeting someone for the first time and hitting it off famously—like they're a long lost friend! Why does that happen? What's at play there?

The fact of the matter is that there are many different kinds of people out there in the world and they all have different styles. You're one style and there are three other primary styles as well. Before I deep dive into how you can navigate all of this, let me first help you with a bit of self-awareness.

You see, it's quite possible that YOU might have rubbed someone the wrong way when you met them for the first time. And it's really not your fault; you are likely just a different style from them. The first step to make these concepts work for you is to understand that these interplays happen all the time with everyone you interact with.

You know that person out networking who is talking "at you" and looking around the room at the same time? Or that other person who you just can't seem to extract yourself from? Or the one who deals his business cards like a poker hand, and then walks to the next group of people to do the same thing?

None of these people are "doing" anything to you—or to anyone else. They are simply being themselves—and their true self is simply a style that is different from yours. Once you can get to a place of objectivity about how this works, you can then begin to talk to different styles more effectively.

I've been working with the concept of styles for over 15 years now, starting when I hired my first coach and then more in-depth when I began teaching my clients. The huge awareness that I gained when understanding different styles really shifted things for me. As a social introvert and also a bit sensitive, I was able to understand that it wasn't about me—it was just their style of dealing with me.

I stopped taking things so personally. I gained greater courage to say the things to them that I needed to say. I was able to choose the right words to say to a particular style very quickly that helped them see that I understood them.

I see the same huge shifts in my clients when they learn about their natural style and the styles of those they interact with. Whether it's their boss, kids, employees, spouse, or prospective clients, they are more effective in motivating people to action once they understand the person's style.

Most important, they are more understanding and forgiving of themselves when they understand their own style. They see their strengths and understand where their tendencies aren't as strong. They can now make decisions to get help in those areas or choose to improve them. It's a tremendously empowering body of work.

I'm also going to ask you to drop most of the "active listening" techniques that you've been taught over the years. You know, the ones where you're supposed to nod when they're speaking? Or say "uh huh?" Or restate what you heard back to them? Sound familiar? Yeah, get rid of all of that.

I know, it seems to fly in the face of most communication seminars out there, but there is a key reason why you should listen to me: brain science. Yep, I'm talkin' about the good ole brain, again. You see, when you're expending that energy and thought process to express those sounds and words, you're literally blocking your ability to really hear what they're saying.

You're using the same neuropathways to receive them as you are to deliver yours. How could you possibly be able to get everything that they're communicating to you if you're so busy generating output? You can't. Even Stephen Covey, author of *The 7 Habits of Highly Effective People,* said "Most people don't listen with the intent to understand, they listen with the intent to reply."

So, skip all of that and shift your focus instead into being a big satellite dish, receiving as much information as you can from them. Only then will you be able to really hear what's important to them and adapt your style in the best way. The great thing is that there are just two primary steps that you need to learn in order to do this:

Step 1: Observe their energy level when they speak.

Are they using demonstrative gestures as they're speaking? Perhaps their delivery is animated and dynamic? Maybe they're more methodical and even-keel with their delivery. Or take long pauses to think and reflect. Maybe you notice that one person isn't talking at all. If you take the time to mirror the energy level of their delivery style, they will likely respond more favorably to what you're trying to get across.

Step 2: Listen to the content of what they're saying.

Are they talking about how important a person is? Or perhaps they're very concerned about being liked by others or how they are perceived. Maybe they're concerned about a particular deadline? Or you might hear them talk about how important it is to progress through all the assigned tasks. By really hearing what's important to them, you can model your response back to them using a similar topic emphasis.

> *"As long as we're waiting for them to be anything better, we will be constantly disappointed."*
> – Marianne Williamson

When it comes to styles, people tend to fall into one group that has a primary concern about relationships and people interactions (Interactors and Supporters) or another group that has a primary concern about getting things done and task accomplishments (Directors and Contemplators).

In the same vein, people tend to fall into a group that has an energetic, demonstrative delivery style with a quick pace (Directors and Interactors) or a group that has a measured delivery style with a moderate pace (Contemplators and Supporters).

Without having to be a mind reader or a fortune teller, you can position your delivery energy in the manner that mirrors theirs and position your content on talking about the things that seem to matter the most to them. By taking this time to talk to them in the way that they talk, you are able to help them hear you better—because you're speaking to them in *their* natural style.

Please don't misunderstand me: I'm not asking you to change who you are. What I'm inviting you to do is to temporarily adjust how and what you deliver so that it lands more powerfully with your listener. You're being a temporary chameleon, able to adjust as you go, and be heard by more people than just those who are your style.

Directors are demonstrative, quick-paced, and task-focused.

Interactors are demonstrative, quick-paced, and relationship-focused.

Supporters are measured, moderately-paced, and relationship-focused.

Contemplators are measured, moderately-paced, and task-focused.

Now, you may be reading this and thinking "hmm, this all sounds familiar. Is it…." NLP? (neurolinguistic programming) No. "Is it…." personality types? (Myers-Briggs/MBTI) No.

It's called DISC and is based on decades of behavioral science research and is a very usable, everyday tool because you can make these observations about other people. You can see behaviors. You can hear what matters to them.

MBTI is more of an indicator of how someone is *internally wired* and DISC is an assessment of how people *behave*. With MBTI there are four letters for each of the sixteen types and with DISC there are four simple primary styles. To understand NLP, you need an in-depth workshop at minimum to begin to understand how to assess people and with DISC it only takes those two simple steps I just taught you—and a little bit of practice.

For those of you who know DISC and are thinking "wait a minute, those names are different from what I learned," I've created the avatars of Director, Interactor, Supporter, and Contemplator because I feel these names paint a clearer picture of the different styles than the original DISC names.

When people feel understood and heard, they feel a greater connection to you. Our biology is affected with more oxytocin, which is that feel-good, connection hormone I mentioned earlier. Those being spoken to in this mindful way feel good and those witnessing the interaction also experience a rise in oxytocin so they feel good too. We're a naturally collaborative species and this level of engagement can strengthen our feeling of community.

You might be wondering how you make a presentation to a small or large group and take these concepts into consideration. The important thing to remember is that if you bring yourself to a more "neutral" place with your content and delivery energy, you will reach more of your audience.

If you're more contemplative, bring your energy level up a bit. If you're very demonstrative, bring it down a notch. If you're presenting a lot of actions and numbers, be sure to pepper in some relationship content. If you're presenting about people, then be sure to bring in some statistics.

Go to www.NoShoutStandOut.com/BookBonus and use the *Wise Why's Worksheet* to learn questions that can help you guess the style of the person you're speaking with. You can also brainstorm what you can say so that you're speaking "their language."

You've heard the phrase that opposites attract? This concept also comes into play when speaking with other people. Often they see something in you or what you're saying that they don't have—and are drawn to you because they want or need it. In other cases, people are drawn to you because they feel an affinity for you or your topic and are a similar style. It's not important to become an expert in identifying styles. What *is* important is to hear what matters to them and include that in your delivery back to them.

And if you're unsure, you can simply bring yourself to a more middle-of-the-road delivery in terms of energy level and content as it will ensure that you're received as openly as possible. This approach works well whether you're presenting to a group or speaking with one person.

Think about the last time someone took this kind of time to connect with you. Can't remember? The busyness of our days often takes us away with it. I believe that Presence is the greatest Present we can give another person. Everyone matters and deserves to be heard. Creating this platform to really receive and hear another person—regardless of their position or beliefs—fosters a level of acceptance that isn't often found elsewhere.

By making this little bit of extra effort, you are creating a "like attracts like" environment because you're taking the time to match them. When doing so, the person leaves the interaction having a very positive impression of you, even though they don't know your effort behind it. This kind of presence with others is a certain way to Stand Out.

Understanding styles is a powerful tool to use whether you're interviewing; speaking to a group; influencing your colleague, team, or boss; talking to your children or partner; or making a proposal to a prospective client. When you adapt your approach to meet your listener, they unconsciously feel more connected to you because they feel heard and sense that you understand them. Regardless of your role, this effort with the other person is what increases your chances of creating great connections.

"My core team is talking with each other more constructively and freely."

Before working with Christine, communication with my key staff members could be a bit reactive and sometimes non-productive. I knew I needed to strengthen my interaction with my core team.

Christine taught us about our styles and how to relate with each other better. They've been able to feel what the customers profiles may be and adjust their approach accordingly.

In just two months, my core team is talking with each other more constructively and freely—which is helping us collaborate better on jobs and when problems arise. I recommend her to any business leader who is looking to motivate their staff.

Rich Lauretta
Spectrum Painting

The Conscious
Conversationalist —
Partnership

The conscious conversationalist — *Partnership*

I believe that technology, as great as it is, is causing our conversation muscles to atrophy. So much of our communication these days seems to be one-way fire-hose output, whether you're getting bombarded with emails from your boss, eNewsletters and promotions, or commercials on TV.

On the surface, especially with the growth of social media, it looks like we're connecting more; yet on a deeper level, we're feeling shouted at and disconnected instead of the original purpose, which was to interact with others. What has happened to this fundamental human connection?

We're foundationally built as collaborative and social beings—it's written in our human biology. Yet some of our workplaces are moving us into solitude and isolation, with much of our work being done behind screens of all sizes—which actually disconnects us and causes stress. It can seem as if we're powerless to operate differently. We, however, are always in choice. If you're feeling this way, too, then there is something you can do about it.

Before you go into doing mode, though, be sure to set reasonable expectations for the outcome. You do not have control over someone else's behavior or actions. You can only operate within your own sphere of influence. So, as you begin practicing the techniques in this section, and this book as a whole, I invite you to keep that top of mind.

The biology of this kind of human connection is also essential to our well-being: it raises oxytocin levels in the body. These hormones are what bond a group together because they feel good and want to belong. They are the antidote to those high cortisol (stress) and dopamine (addiction) levels I mentioned earlier.

In her book *The Fear Cure*, Lissa Rankin, MD, ties the excessive cortisol levels in our bodies to our fight or flight mechanism being "on" all the time. This kind of conversational connection literally contributes to the stronger physical, emotional, and mental health of those involved by turning off fight or flight.

The opportunity you have as you prepare to have these individual conversations is to understand that others may not have the same affinity or skill for conversing as you may have. Also, especially if they are in the younger generation, they may not even have learned very much about how to have constructive conversations because they've only experienced this world of technology and output in their generation. Accept them for where they are and do your best to interact with them in the way you're learning here.

When I first started networking as a social introvert, I really had no qualms about talking to people because I am not shy. Yet I realized over time that I was doing so much networking and not seeing the results I thought I would be getting. I got swamped with trying to keep track of all of my follow-ups and I was feeling exhausted—not to mention unmotivated to pick up that 100-pound phone to make follow up calls.

Once I created this conversation method, I saw things turn around for me. I began to gain so many more qualified leads and have so many more meaningful conversations. Today, my network has grown very large—and full of kindred spirits. I am doing less networking and seeing more results—my ROTI (Return On Time Investment) finally came around by using these tools.

As you prepare for any conversation, refresh your memory on the first three principles of this book:
- **Purpose**—what do you want to accomplish with this interaction?
- **Passion**—how can you message yourself in a compelling way?
- **Presence**—what is your style and how can you adapt to theirs?

Conversations are like mini-meetings: they have a beginning, a middle, and an end. Oftentimes our uncertainty about networking is that we don't know what is going to happen or what a person is going to say. Conversations can be messy, yet with architecture like a mini-meeting, you can take a bit of control over how you intend it to go.

Conversations flow the best when you think of each of the three steps taking up 1/3 of the total meeting time. If your meeting is 30 minutes, then spend 10 minutes on each stage. If it's 60 minutes, then spend 20 minutes on each stage. If you're networking, then it might need to be five minutes for each stage because of your time constraint.

> *"Mindful listening and speaking will make it easier for us to build a stronger community."*
> – *Thich Nhat Hanh*

In the first stage of the conversation, your focus is on them and their expertise or interests. In the second stage, you take the opportunity to share about you. In the last stage, you recap what you heard and agree on next steps or actions to take.

It's that middle stage that often hiccups us. We don't know how to turn the conversation back to us without feeling pushy, interruptive, or icky. Now that you've learned how to share your purpose and your messaging, that stage should start feeling more comfortable.

If you invite people to have a one-on-one with you after meeting them when networking, the same architecture applies. As people of service, we often give the entire time over to the person we wanted to meet. This method helps you bring the conversation back to you, if you need to, so that you have an equitable exchange of information and resources.

That leads me to share a formula to use within the conversation as well. I like to use the acronym A.S.K.: Acknowledge, State, and Know. Acknowledge what you heard or observed; State your desired outcome or the situation; and Know by asking a question to evoke a response. This formula is modeled after those used in conflict resolution and non-violent communication practices.

Here's a multi-purpose example that I like to call "managing expectations"—it's a way to help people understand how the conversation is going to go. When people know at the beginning what the "agenda" for the conversation is going to be, then it helps put them at ease. You can use this networking, in one-on-ones, or even hosting a group meeting:

Start by saying something like *"Jane, thank you for your time today. I'd like to learn a little bit more about you, your work and your company, share some things about me, my experience, and my needs, and then we can decide together what our next steps—if any—will be. How does that sound?"*

The "Acknowledge" was thanking Jane for her time. The "State" was outlining the parameter of the conversation. The "Know" was asking Jane how that all sounded. That's it, short, sweet, and succinct!

This approach is a powerful tool because it helps people understand the architecture of your time together and it puts them at ease because they know what to expect. It may feel a little bit curt and short to some of you who strongly value being relational with people. What I know from experience is that when I'm feeling a little anxious about initiating the interaction, this model helps me stay focused. When I'm nervous, I tend to ramble on a bit, and this helps keep me on track.

In addition, those of us who are in service to others have a tendency not to ask for what we want and need and this formula ensures that we don't forget to. It's a formula that is applicable to most styles of people, so it is very effective no matter whom you're talking to.

Here's a networking example:

"Well, Mike, I can tell that you're really passionate about your work. I'd like to chat further with you so we can find

out more about each other's business and see if we can make connections for each other. Would you like to connect again on a phone chat early next week?"

The "Acknowledge" is stating an observation about Mike. The "State" is telling Mike you'd like to talk further. The "Know" is asking whether Mike is interested in chatting further. When you A.S.K. in the moment, it makes your follow-up so much easier.

I'm on a one-woman mission to reinstate the art of conversation so those human connections can be made in any work environment:

Business leaders. True employee engagement doesn't come from broad-scale company communications. It starts with an engaged conversation by first-level supervisors and managers to connect with each individual within their team or department. It starts with you having individual conversations with your direct reports and helping them understand their connection to the greater company mission and vision. It starts with you understanding the styles of your team members so that you can speak to them in their style and be better heard.

Job seekers. Career opportunities don't come from relying solely on the online application process. They come from you initiating a conversation with one person to relay what you're looking for. They come from you having a clear understanding of your purpose and finding the jobs that most closely match your calling. They come from you respectfully following up and following through with the people who gave you their time, attention, and connections.

Small business owners. Prospective customers and clients don't only come from your website, social media posts, or email newsletter blasts. They also come from your purposeful interaction to be a resource with current clients and while networking. They come from referrals of delighted customers and clients who can't help but sing your praises because they feel so connected with your Purpose—all because they were treated in such a kind, engaged, and solution-focused way.

Think of a conversation as multiple, small A.S.K.s happening back and forth—a bit like a tennis match. Biting it off in smaller chunks makes it flow more naturally, feel less like a confrontation, and gains more information along the way.

The magic of the A.S.K. formula lies in the Acknowledge and the Know. "Acknowledge" diffuses any potential feelings of confrontation, which sets a safe tone for the conversation to occur. "Know" invites a response, which keeps the conversation flowing.

As was discussed about speaking your Purpose and using micro-messaging, creating a platform for yourself in which to ask is also a specific tool to get what you want. It communicates specifically to the Universe what you desire and it enables other Universal conduits—people—to help make it happen.

In addition, you're empowering yourself with these techniques because you're creating the space for it to happen—and you're designing the opportunity to ask for what you want and need. Most kindred spirits are more than happy to help us, but they aren't mind readers—we have to tell them how they can help us.

Go to www.NoShoutStandOut.com/BookBonus and use the *Fruitful 1-on-1 Worksheet* to learn more ways to be a resource in private conversations. Thinking through your approach ahead of time can help you come across more comfortable and confident.

"You've got to put your ask out there," whether you're leading a team, looking for a job, cleaning up after your family, vying for a promotion, or marketing your business. As people of service, we'd like for others to notice what we need—like we often do for others. For lots of different reasons, they don't always attune themselves to us like we do for others. Having conversations in this efficient and concise way will help you not assume and get what you want.

When you're able to articulate yourself to others, you're creating that "like attracts like" energy so that your vision of what you want can come to you. This energy shows up in any conversation you might have in your business, life, or career.

By taking a personal approach and using the conversation as your communication medium, you will stand out and get noticed. Now that you are articulating your purpose and using compelling messaging, you can use them to be even more effective within these conversations. You'll have the information you want and need and can rest in the knowledge that you initiated the steps within your sphere of influence along the way.

It's not always easy having or initiating these conversations. Yet, the only way to grow your skill is to practice, practice, practice. That's why I've created the Participation section next, to show you how to take these techniques into real-life situations. You've learned a lot so far; now it's time to put it into inspired action.

"Helped me feel less emotional and less stressed."

Christine and I worked together to address the most pressing issue of me managing the relationship with my new manager.

Christine's keen sense of alignment with an individual's spirit enables her to meet you where you are. Through some of the activities and role playing I was able to acquire new communication skills that are useful in every aspect of my life.

The conversation model helped me feel less emotional and less stressed. My conversations are now quite manageable, which helps me to be more intentional and clear. I highly recommend working with her and am certain you will find the results extremely satisfying.

Shanna Hawes
Project Management Consultant

The Successful Implementer —
Participation

The successful implementer —
Participation

*I*n this fast-paced world, it's easy to have good intentions but often harder to actually implement things. I like to take a systematic approach to trying new things and I find that also works for my creative-thinking clients.

The ideas and examples found here are both real-world applications of what you've learned and different approaches and perspectives—including examples beyond just networking. Remember what I said at the beginning of this book: these techniques work everywhere in your life, not just when networking.

For many of the examples here, I've given you a special gift of $10.00 off my digital programs that apply to certain topics. The programs are a low-cost investment, ranging from only $11 to $65 after the discount. You can save up to $60.00 if you try them all.

Inspired action:

You may feel a little overwhelmed with all this information right now. I would hate it if you put this book down and took no action on what you've learned. What one small step can you take right now? Which approach seems the most manageable? Do that one.

Better yet, plan out when and how you're going to implement these concepts. Maybe you work better with an accountability buddy. It's best to align your actions with your natural style and strength, so take some time to lay it all out to set yourself up for success.

To learn more about taking inspired action that's aligned with you and your purpose, you can go to www.NoShoutStandOut.com/BookBonus *and use the $10 coupon there to purchase my "Your Spirit at Work" guidebook for only $29 (normally $39). It also contains additional visual tools and worksheets that support the techniques in this book.*

Networking strategy:

In the small business world, I say that networking often feels a lot like bad dating: we get together and enjoy each other's company, but we leave not knowing who's calling who. I've seen some really bad meetings happen in my corporate days as well; it was a rare manager who ran a good one. Your best approach is a well-thought out one.

Networking isn't a place you go, it's a thing you do. Just because "everyone" is going to that networking event doesn't mean it's the best place for you to go.

Who do you want to meet? Why do you want to meet them (Purpose)? Where are you going to invite them (A.S.K.)? Where do these people hang out? Go there or reach out individually.

Whether you're in job search or networking for your business, these critical questions can help you be super-efficient and effective in using the time that you spend networking.

What are your strengths? Do you feel confident going to a large networking event? If not, then you aren't going to come across confident. Sure, you might be able to benefit from learning to be more confident when networking in large groups, but that will take time to develop. Determine your training plan there and begin to work towards it.

In the meantime, specifically identify who you want to meet, prepare your message, and then build your net-work. You might begin calling people you already know and feel comfortable with. Simply tell them who you want to meet and why, and ask them if they know anyone they'd be willing to connect you to. If you don't prefer the phone, then invite them to have coffee with you and you can talk with them there. That's networking, too. Choose what works for you.

As one of my coaches says, "All Ways Work."

Networking tactics:

If you are choosing to make networking events a part of your marketing activities, then use the same approach as identifying your networking strategy: leverage your natural strengths. If you're on the quiet side, you likely prefer having fewer but deeper conversations with individual people. If you're more outgoing, you will likely want to get to as many people there as you can. If you're intuitive like me, then you also likely trust that you'll end up meeting the right people along the way. Does this sound about right?

Regardless of your style, when you arrive at your networking event and park your car, take a moment to breathe and center yourself. Think about the goals you have and your purpose for coming to this event. Decide what you'd like to get out of your time there. For example, if you're a speaker, then perhaps it is finding a lead for a speaking event. Or maybe you're holding a class or event and are looking for attendees.

After you think about your intention for this event, walk in to the room and pause a moment. While it may initially feel conspicuous, it actually gives you a little time to survey the room. This is time for you to tap into your intuition and walk towards a group of people that you feel drawn to. When you arrive, pause until they're done talking, and then ask "May I join you?" Chances are, they're there to network as well and will welcome you into their group and begin to introduce each other.

There's no need to force yourself to "work the room" when you have your goals in mind. You may end up only talking to a handful of people. Use your power of connection when you're speaking with individuals and bridge the ones that feel like kindred spirits into the next step with you. Be aware that most people are going to want to talk with other people—so note when you sense they are ready to move on. When they do, just repeat the process of surveying the room and using your intuition to move to the next group.

The bridge:

If you're like me and don't prefer to pick up the phone to make cold phone calls, then this bridge concept might be for you. In every interaction or conversation, I make sure that I know what I want next so that I can "bridge" the person into it seamlessly.

If I'm networking, I know that I'll invite people I want to know better into a phone conversation—so I ask them right there at the networking event. If I'm emailing someone and want to get them on the phone, I use the A.S.K. formula to invite them to have a phone chat.

When I gain their permission, it makes it easier for me to pick up the phone because they are expecting my call. It also makes it more likely that they'll pick up the phone because they're expecting my call.

The bridge concept works in every interaction, not just to overcome using the phone. Yet, in order to use it, you must have thought through where you want to take them. It doesn't have to be a "sell"; you can simply be looking to help them. If you're interviewing, for example, you can ask what the next steps are and whether/how to best follow-up during the interviewing cycle. Once you decide what you want, the bridge invitation becomes so very easy.

> *To learn more about using the phone effectively and comfortably, you can go to* <u>www.NoShout StandOut.com/BookBonus</u> *and use the $10 coupon there to purchase my "Dialing for Dollars" class for only $11 (normally $21).*

Time-blocking:

Depending on your position or circumstance, you may need to modify this system for you. At minimum, note the general parameters I share here and use them in the system you create for yourself.

When setting up conversations, I find that blocking out a group of hours in a day helps me focus and get them done. It makes it super easy to invite people because you already have the time set aside on your calendar. That block of time gives me the parameter to take a look at the purpose of the conversation, the message I want to convey, and the person that I'll be speaking with.

While this example is one for a business owner who is marketing herself, how could you make this time-block/visual approach work for you? If you're a business leader, perhaps you have a team meeting on the calendar once per week. Could you enhance your team interaction by meeting individually with each person at least once per month? If this feels feasible and constructive to building collaboration and productivity, then make appointments with each of your team members.

If you're in job search, set aside a block of hours where you're researching your connections on LinkedIn and making a list of people you want to call for informational interviews. Have a few set times in your calendar so it's easy to invite the person into one of your time slots. While in person is best, the phone is definitely effective

> *"What you do is proof of what you believe."*
> – Simon Sinek

for this. You might even consider free video services like Skype, Zoom, or Google+ Hangout to have the interview in order to up your effectiveness to 65% because you're now seeing facial expressions.

If you are on a project in your workplace, how could you begin to connect with your project leader or fellow members better? Could you put some time on your schedule to chat with them or even grab coffee or lunch with them? Check in with them to see how things are going on their end of the project. This kind of intentional activity is leadership. If you're looking to be seen without selling yourself, it's the perfect way to start making a positive impact on those around you.

To learn more about creating efficiencies in your business or life, you can go to www.NoShout StandOut.com/BookBonus *and use the $10 coupon there to purchase my "7 Super Simple Business Secrets to Earn More, Do Less, and Make a Bigger Difference" eWorkbook for only $11 (normally $21).*

Following-up:

When was the last time that you received a notecard from someone for no particular reason? Or an email from someone that told you about an event they thought you'd be interested in? Or a resource that someone thought you could benefit from? That someone could be you.

This approach of keeping in touch with kindred spirits is a sure way to stand out. These are referral sources, former clients, prospective clients, former bosses and colleagues, joint venture partners, former teachers and professors, future strategic alliances, and the list can go on. I once heard that every person that you know, knows

250 people that they would at least be willing to send a personal email to on your behalf.

By creating a systematic approach to staying in touch with those people who are your advocates and allies, you are keeping your access to those 250 people alive. If that sounds a bit self-serving, yes, it is! AND, in the process, you are providing them value with what you choose to send them in order to stay in touch.

Some people want and need that reciprocation, some people don't. Go back and review the section on styles and you'll see that "I" and "S" styles prefer relational connection and "D" and "C" styles prefer more rational connection. So, take the time to really understand who these folks are and be a resource to them *in a way that matters to them.*

An excellent resource for creating your own communication plan is the book *7 Levels of Communication* by Michael Maher. It is an easy read because it's positioned as a fiction story, yet is packed full of usable systems. While written for the real estate professional, it applies to everyone.

> *To learn more about following up effectively and comfortably, you can go to www.NoShoutStand Out.com/BookBonus and use the $10 coupon there to purchase my "The Fortune is in the Follow-up" class for only $11 (normally $21).*

Selling yourself:

I happen to believe that "If you market really well, you don't have to sell." Sales is really just providing a solution to a need. For many business owners, I see them attempting to "sell" their entire business. Instead, they really only need to develop two to three strong micro-messages. Once they get solid messaging to the "who" with the "benefit" that applies to each of those services, they will gain more people's interest.

If you're "selling" yourself as a job candidate, the same approach applies. You likely tend to speak to your entire skill set on a cover letter and/or in an interview. Instead, choose your top three strengths/skills and determine how an employer specifically benefits from each of them. Then speak to just those three in your cover letter and in the interview.

Most candidates talk a lot about *everything* they can do and the listener can get lost in all of those words. By positioning yourself as a specific solution to the company's need using those two to three strengths, you'll have a better chance to make it through to the next round.

In all cases, speaking your Purpose is a persuasive sales tool as well. Whether you use it during the marketing phase or the sales phase, it can help distinguish your kindred spirits pretty quickly. Even if they don't want to buy or hire you, your expression of your Purpose makes you more memorable and they keep a part of you in their mind share. If they feel you share the same motivation and core values, the likelihood is much greater that a sale will be made down the road.

Integrate speaking your Purpose, micro-messaging, A.S.K., time-blocking, and the bridge to create a seamless sales approach. Opportunities flow where your systems go.

> *To learn more about creating a sales process that feels right for you, you can go to* <u>www.NoShout StandOut.com/BookBonus</u> *and use the $10 coupon there to purchase my "Softer Side of Selling" class for only $11 (normally $21).*

Choosing the best conversation medium:

Before you start your conversations, go back to the communication statistics in the beginning of this book. Remember that the most effective conversations happen in person, with 100% of what you intend getting across. Your second most effective option is video/Skype (65%); your third most effective option is phone/audio (30%); and your least effective option is email/text (7%).

If you're a business owner sending off a proposal via email, stop a minute. How possible is a meeting instead, either in person or via Skype? For something that important, you want to have as much communication effectiveness in your court as possible. Email is only 7% effective because it uses words alone.

If you're confirming logistics, texting or email is probably all you need. If you're seeking understanding of a situation, and you can't meet in person, you might consider video/Skype so you can at least see their facial expressions as you navigate the situation together.

The phone is a great way to find a mutual day/time for an appointment, so you avoid the wasted time of emailing back and forth.

Set yourself up for success by choosing the appropriate medium for what you want to accomplish.

A.S.K. in email:

While the A.S.K. method is tremendously effective when speaking to others, it can also work well in email. Stick to the A.S.K. formula in an email and you'll begin seeing that medium work much more efficiently for you. The formula works for all styles, so you can ensure that it will land well with most everyone. Emails become easier to write and, with that magical "Know" question at the end, you'll get back the information that you're looking for.

Conversation vs. Communication:

It's easy to send a mass email or newsletter or ask a general question of a group. The problem is that it doesn't land personally with the individuals on the receiving end. Communication seems to have morphed into complete output. Conversation is engagement of an individual. Focusing on this approach certainly isn't the fastest—but I believe it is the most effective method to engage others.

In corporate, I saw a similar mass-communication tactic often being used by managers of teams. They would address issues to the group during a staff meeting instead of speaking specifically to the person(s) who were causing the issues. This instilled two things to those teams: that no one really had to worry about being reprimanded because the team always took the heat; and "to each his own" because each thought, "Why should I take the heat for the person who is causing the issues?" Separateness, not connection.

Find the connection through conversation with individuals. Be curious about them and ask questions as to what they're facing. Be sincere when connecting them to a resource or responding to their concerns. Help them troubleshoot options. In this way— through that conversation—you will be remembered and valued.

Visual tools:

As a creative-thinking business owner, I'm also a very visual learner and doer. I may jot things down on a to-do list, but they really don't get done unless I move them onto my calendar. While I do use an electronic calendar, I also have a wall calendar where I use different colored dry-erase markers to represent different business activities.

When I plan my marketing or project activities, I use colorful sticky notes. I have a system where, once I've planned things out, I move the small sticky note "tasks" onto a hard-copy planner. While I do use an online calendar, this physical weekly planner motivates me more because it's in front of me no matter what I'm working on.

Entrepreneur target market focus:

For entrepreneurs, I suggest they focus on two primary micro-messages, which also typically means the same number of target markets. Quite honestly, especially for solopreneurs, this breadth of focus is as much as they can feasibly take on in terms of supporting marketing activity.

If you try to be all things to all people, you'll end up being no one to everyone. You must choose the groups who really light you up to serve; or choose the groups who really want that special service you offer. The better known you become to that group of people or for that service, the greater traction you'll gain the most quickly.

To learn more about creating your own manage-able activity plan in a visually appealing way, you can go to www.NoShoutStandOut.com/Book-Bonus and use the $10 coupon there to purchase my "Wealth Harvest" program for only $65 (nor-mally $75).

Body language:

Though I'm not a body language expert, I'd be remiss not to at least give it a mention in a book called *You don't have to shout to Stand Out*. I do find that it helps to be aware of how I'm carrying myself when I speak with or approach someone.

As a swing dancer, I've adopted good posture in the process of learning to dance. I learned dance as an adult. Think about taking an adult dance or improv class. Or simply bring a bit more self-awareness about your carriage while you're walking, sitting, or working out. You may want to read a bit about neurolinguistic pro-gramming or NLP, which helps you better understand facial expressions and body language. It also teaches you how to use it in response to what someone else does, which can put the person you're talking to at ease.

Amy Cuddy wrote a book called *Presence* and in it she highlights her research on how "power posing" can influence your brain chemistry. It's no wonder I found something else about brain science to use in this book!

In short, when holding power poses for a mere two minutes, her research showed a decline in cortisol (the stress hormone) in the body and a rise in testosterone (the confidence hormone). The people who used these poses came across more calm and confident—and all of them were "chosen" for a job during the job interview part of the research by a panel who didn't know some interviewees had used power poses before going in.

Just like the other pointers in this book, body language works the best in person with others. However, it can also work powerfully on the other side of the phone, video, or email when used in preparation for those kinds of interactions. If you feel conspicuous doing power poses at work, find a bathroom stall or do it as you're getting out of your car on the way in. It's proven that it works. You might even get up and walk around when you're having a phone conversation so your natural energy comes through.

"I am now confident when I speak."

Christine helped me outline the areas where I needed the most guidance, prioritized them, worked with me and kept me accountable. She makes it so easy and actionable. We worked together on messaging, marketing bridges, and sales conversations.

I am now confident when I speak whether it is networking or a meeting with a potential client or an engaged client to renew their contract. Christine also made me realize the value I bring to my clients and structured pricing accordingly.

Christine even walked me through situations where I was not comfortable. I HIGHLY recommend Christine. She has made a tremendous difference not only in my business but in me personally.

Cheryl Mucha
CFO Your Way

Go Forth
and Be Heard —
and be You!

Now Go Forth and Be Heard — *and be You!*

*B*eing drawn to serve others is an amazing gift. You've seen in this book how you can leverage your natural style in order to inspire interest and create connections through networking conversations. These approaches work whether you are on the quiet side like me or are more outgoing. As different styles, we have the opportunity to meet in the middle.

The understanding of introverts is becoming more mainstream, thanks to Susan Cain who wrote *Quiet: The Power of Introverts in a World that Can't Stop Talking*. I'm really glad for that greater understanding. However, I'm also seeing groups of introverts come together declaring a sort of "I am who I am" position against everyone else. This kind of approach separates us instead of connects us. As you know by now, I'm all about connection.

I love that introverts are finding it easier to find supportive groups of like-mindedness, but not all of those groups are supporting an approach to find a way to connect with others not like them.

No matter what style you are, you can't expect others to

be mind readers. We sometimes have to teach others how we want to be treated. In order to do that, we have the responsibility to articulate ourselves.

This book is a tool I'm offering you for just that purpose. Not only might you have gained a better understanding about who you are in this book, but you now also have specific tools and techniques you can use to find a way to connect with others not like you. I believe it's our responsibility to find the place where we can connect.

You've heard the biology factors I've shared in this book, right? The oxytocin boost we get by connecting with other humans not only increases our collaboration and cooperation, it also combats the high levels of cortisol that stress causes. I believe that lack of human connection will be the downfall of our society. The belief of separateness will continue to create a huge gap. It's okay that we're all different—yet how can we be different, together?

I believe that everybody matters and deserves to be heard. Conversations are the place where that connection can be made, whether we agree with the other person or not. All of us can leverage our natural style and take the time to connect with others in this conversational way. The world is cheated without your voice in it—and will be a lesser place without these connections that you are so naturally equipped to make.

When you gain clarity around your Purpose and articulate it; when you declare who you help and how they benefit; when you meet people in their style; and when you create the space to connect in conversation—you are empowering yourself to be heard. When you declare your intentions in this way, the Universe is supporting you by operating within your practical sphere of influence in a meaningful, intuitive way.

Giving yourself these platforms and systems to interact with others in order to have these constructive conversations will set you up to strengthen your vital conversation muscle. And, you know what? You're going to help them strengthen theirs as well. They will see something in you and your approach that is compelling and interesting to them—that some of them will want to emulate. In the process, you'll be finding out the information you need and also be giving them the platform to be heard in your conversation so that you can see what you can do for them.

You have the power to reinstate the art of conversation to bring these human connections back. Your conversations are the bridge between the amazingness of new technology and the time-proven approach of human interaction. Technology will inevitably continue to evolve. We can ensure that how we deal with people will continue to evolve along with it.

We cannot do without either one, so our opportunity is to use them both in powerful ways. By participating in these conversations, you will help reignite our human biology of connection and collaboration so you can make a bigger difference. Help others be heard and you, too, will be heard.

You don't have to shout to Stand Out.

"*Let's all meet where we can relate at the highest level and shed the veil of separateness.*

Let's see each other as individual threads in the colorful tapestry of the Divine: each of us playing our individual, unique part and knowing that everyone else must, too.

Difference is good, it is important, it is essential. We have an opportunity to remember that, honor that, and accept everyone for the unique thread that they are.

Because, without them, the tapestry wouldn't be as brilliant or as strong."

Christine Clifton

Quick Links to Christine's Resources

Join our community by registering here:
www.NoShoutStandOut.com

Claim your Book Bonuses:
www.NoShoutStandOut/BookBonus

Join our Facebook Group:
www.facebook.com/groups/NoShoutStandOut

Get some additional support:
www.MindfulBusinessMatters.com/Shop

Check out my website:
www.MindfulBusinessMatters.com

Connect with me on LinkedIn:
www.linkedin.com/in/cclifton

Connect with me on Twitter:
www.twitter.com/NoShoutStandOut

Schedule a free chat with Christine:
www.ChatWithChristine.com

Acknowledgments

I knew exactly what I was getting into when I chose to self-publish this book. I did much research and weighed many options. Then I took a leap of faith….. along with these Rock Stars:

Bruce Clifton created the 'word cloud' image that then became the book cover. A fantastic graphic artist and a lovely brother, he's rocked his company Bullseye Visuals for over 30 years now.

Marty Marsh has been a dear friend of mine for over 5 years and continually rocks my world with his diversity of skills. From a Law of Attraction coach to an email marketing master, he designed this book inside and out.

Paul Zelizer crept into my world on Facebook somehow, we all know how that goes. As I watched him, I saw great integrity and alignment. The co-founder of *Wisdompreneurs,* he helped me rock my book launch messaging and tactics.

Karen Bomm 'got me' in the first 5 minutes of talking with her about my book. She rocks at channeling the author so the right SEO words are found that align with the person first and the internet second – and not sacrifice the power of either.

My fellow authors who agreed to read my book and give me feedback and a review. They know the trials and tribulations of publishing, regardless of which method you choose. I'm so appreciative of their time and support:

- **Chris Curran,** Founder, Fractal Recording, Author of "Leap Beyond Your Limits"
- **Bryan Kramer,** CEO at PureMatter, TED Speaker, Best Selling Author of "Human to Human #H2H" and "Shareology"
- **Bonnie Marcus,** Author of "The Politics of Promotion"
- **Kathy Ryan,** Founder, Pinnacle Leadership Institute, Author of "You Have to Say the Words"
- **Doug Sandler,** Author of "Nice Guys Finish First"
- **Maria Semple,** CEO, The Prospect Finder, Author of "Magnify Your Business"
- **Jennifer Urezzio,** Author of "Soul Language" and "A Little Book of Prayers"

Alyssa Peek has a very special way of coaxing the richness of a woman through her photographs. It took me two months to accept that was really me in my pictures because she rocked her lens so well.

And, finally, my introvert's short list of close friends who always have my back: **Sylvia, Jen, Steve, Dawn, Stephanie, Gene,** and **Ann.** Get ready, guys—the next book is already being written.

What's next?

Thank you so much for taking the time to read my take on these networking skills and approaches. As you've gathered, I'm passionate about connecting people to resources. I'm equally passionate about helping them connect to their calling and intuition. I want everyone to shine their bright light into the world so they can help more people. As a result, I'll be deciding which of these two books to focus on first:

The Secrets of Service Selling:
Create a steady stream of loyal clients

Ignite your Inner Leader:
Gain the clarity and confidence you crave

Just email me at Christine@ChristineClifton.com to tally your vote!

References

Clifton, Christine. Your Spirit at Work: Bring more of You through what you Do so your vision comes True. Madison: Mindful Business Matters, 2014.

Cuddy, Amy. Presence: Bringing Your Boldest Self to Your Biggest Challenges. Boston: Little, Brown and Company, 2015.

DISC Profile. https://www.discinsights.com/disc-history#.VqT6FfkrLIU

Maher, Michael. 7L: The Seven Levels of Communication: Go From Relationships to Referrals. Dallas: Benbella Books, 2014.

Palmer, Parker J. Let Your Life Speak: Listening for the Voice of Vocation. New York: John Wiley & Sons, 2000.

Rankin, Lissa. The Fear Cure: Cultivating Courage as Medicine for the Body, Mind, and Soul. New York: Hay House, 2015.

Sinek, Simon. Start with Why: How Great Leaders Inspire Everyone to Take Action. New York. Portfolio/Penguin, 2009.

Sinek, Simon. Leaders Eat Last: Why Some Teams Pull Together and Others Don't. New York: Portfolio/Penguin, 2013.

Slim, Pamela. Body of Work: Finding the Thread That Ties Your Story Together. New York: Portfolio/Penguin, 2013.

Birdwhistell, Raymond:
http://www.culturalequity.org/alanlomax/ce_alanlomax_profile_birdwhistell.php

About the Author

Christine Clifton is a possibilities thinker. She's a collaborative rainmaker for professional services firms: teaching them how to have fruitful conversations that create connections with the right people and resources. As a quiet entrepreneur, Christine founded *Mindful Business Matters* and enjoys inspirational speaking and writing to bring her voice into the world.

When she took her leap of faith into entrepreneurship after a 20-year management career, she realized she didn't know how to network like a pro. She made some mistakes communicating; yet learned how to have connected networking conversations so she could help more people and grow her business. She now teaches her quiet power techniques so other relational business-people can avoid the energy drain of promoting themselves and the "feast and famine" of service entrepreneurship.

By showing up authentically in their work, introverts or extraverts can better align what they do with who they are and Thrive!

41442652R10072

Made in the USA
Middletown, DE
12 March 2017